# Counseling and Guidance
# in the Schools

# Counseling and Guidance in the Schools

*Three Exemplary Guidance Approaches*

Garry R. Walz and Thomas I. Ellis, Editors

*Reference & Resource Series*

nea PROFESSIONAL LIBRARY
National Education Association
Washington, D.C.

Printing History
    First Printing:    March 1992

**Note**

The opinions expressed in this publication should not be construed as representing the policy or position of the National Education Association. Materials published by the NEA Professional Library are intended to be discussion documents for educators who are concerned with specialized interests of the profession.

**Library of Congress Cataloging-in-Publication Data**

Counseling and guidance in the schools: three exemplary guidance approaches
    / Garry R. Walz and Thomas I. Ellis, editors.
        p.   cm. — (Reference & resource series)
        Includes bibliographical references (p.      ).
        ISBN 0-8106-1541-X
        1.   Personnel service in education — United States. I. Walz, Garry Richard. II. Ellis, Thomas I. III. Series.
    LB1027.5.C652   1992
    371.4'0973—dc20                           91-34754
                                                                  CIP

# CONTENTS

## The Editors

Garry R. Walz is Professor of Education and Director of the ERIC/CAPS Center at the University of Michigan, Ann Arbor.

Thomas I. Ellis, formerly an Information Specialist at the ERIC/CAPS Center, is now an Instructor at Wayne State University, Detroit.

## The Advisory Panel

Vanessa S. Baugh, Counselor, Penn-Trafford School District, Trafford, Pennsylvania

James Boehlke, Guidance Counselor, Washington High School, Two Rivers, Wisconsin

Chari Campbell, Assistant Professor of Counselor Education, University of South Carolina, Columbia

Audry L. Lynch, Head Guidance Counselor, Bernal Intermediate School, Oak Grove School District, San Jose, California

Meredith Monteville, Counselor, Aiea Intermediate School, Aiea, Hawaii

William A. Poppen, Professor of Educational and Counseling Psychology, University of Tennessee, Knoxville

Carl F. Rak, Assistant Professor, Cleveland State University, Ohio

Leslie A. Rothman, Counselor, Union Hill High School, Union City, New Jersey

Jan Schneider, Counselor, Francis Howell School District, St. Charles, Missouri

Steve Zuber, Counselor, Eisenhower High School, Yakima, Washington

# INTRODUCTION

The search for quality practice and program guidance resources is a never-ending one. Journals are replete with descriptions of this or that practice innovation. New programmatic guidance designs tried out by schools are increasingly being presented in commercial publications. Still the thirst for quality guidance ideas and resources goes on unabated. Probably two reasons explain this unmet need for such resources. First, despite the plenitude of "self-nominated" quality guidance resources, practitioners have a difficult time discriminating between real quality and more "also-ran" approaches. Seldom is the information about a given practice/program innovation complete enough to be discriminating. Replication of the procedures (frequently glowingly described), given the paucity of how-to information provided, is also difficult. A second difficulty is the focus of the literature on guidance innovations. The literature may be so broad and pervasive in scope and so demanding of new elements and resources that its adoptability by a school system is highly problematical. The reverse is also true. The innovation may be so focused on a small population subset or of interest to only a small segment of the client population (e.g., counseling students with AIDS) that for most school counselors the topic is only of general interest. Clearly, what is needed is hard to find—adoptable innovations with proven track records that speak to the needs of a large segment of school guidance programs. And that is what this monograph is all about.

After a review of dozens of guidance programs, we selected three for inclusion in our Crème de la Crème Series—*the best of the best* (ERIC/CAPS Publications 1990). Our two main criteria for inclusion in the series are that a program (1) have a solid conceptual foundation and (2) be field validated through extensive and successful use in school programs across the country. The first three programs included in the Crème de la

Crème Series and described in this monograph meet the criteria for solid conceptual foundation and extensive field validation extremely well. That is why we call them exemplary.

Readers are encouraged to review each program separately and to reflect on its merits and its possible use in their schools. Perhaps the best use of the programs, however, is not as three separate guidance program innovations, but rather as three programs that when integrated together can produce a synergistic outcome in the form of a comprehensive guidance program that attends to the needs of all students especially well and provides an inviting and nurturing environment that builds effective behaviors and positive attitudes for both students and staff.

Readers who find any or all of the program descriptions contained here attractive will want to pursue their interest by reading the monographs devoted to each of the three guidance programs. These publications (Gysbers 1990; Myrick and Myrick 1990; Purkey and Schmidt 1990) provide more information about individual programs and how to implement them in a given school situation. Particularly useful are the reports by program users on how to successfully implement them and pitfalls to avoid in early adoption and adaptation.

Read and enjoy. If we can be of any assistance, please do not hesitate to contact us. Providing useful information is what we are all about.

—Garry R. Walz

Chapter 1

# THE COMPREHENSIVE GUIDANCE PROGRAM MODEL

by **Norman C. Gysbers,** Professor of Education, University of Missouri, Columbia

*One word that most school counselors would like to see banished from their job descriptions is "ancillary," as in "ancillary school services." Too often, counselors have been perceived as inessential support personnel outside the mainstream of the educational process, whose role is limited primarily to dealing with "problem" students or to intervening in crises. For the rest of the time, counselors are expected to do anything else that their principals can think up for them: some vocational guidance, some psychological testing, some personal, social, or academic counseling, and, above all, a great deal of paperwork. Moreover, most counselors are accustomed to having new tasks heaped on them when they least expect it, because of the perception that they, unlike teachers, have time to spare. And so counselors tend to be subjected to an ever-growing laundry list of miscellaneous duties over which they have little control. This marginality of the school counselor's role is neither necessary nor desirable.*

*One solution to the closely linked problems of marginality, busywork, demoralization, and consequent diminished effectiveness of counselors is a programmatic design. Norman Gysbers' Comprehensive Guidance Program Model reintegrates guidance into the curriculum and redefines the coun-*

9

*selor's role and duties in the context of the overall guidance program. It aims to set up a guidance curriculum to integrate the work of school counselors into the educational mainstream.*

## OVERVIEW

During the late 1950s, the 1960s, and the early 1970s, the counselor-clinical services approach to guidance dominated professional theory, training, and practice. In the schools, those who adopted this approach emphasized the counselor and counseling. Administratively, guidance was part of pupil personnel services. The focus was on a position (counselor) and a process (counseling), not on a program (guidance).

Guidance in the schools did not begin that way, however. It began as vocational guidance with an emphasis on occupational selection and placement. But in the early 1920s, a more clinically oriented approach, which stressed counseling, began to emerge. While concern for occupational selection and placement was present, a greater concern was expressed for personal adjustment. Thus the era of guidance for adjustment had begun.

During the late 1920s and early 1930s, the beginnings of the services approach to organizing guidance in the schools appeared. Counseling continued to be featured as the dominant process; only now it was one of a number of services. By this time, too, the traditional way of describing guidance as a service with three aspects—vocational, educational, and personal-social—was well established. Finally, in the 1950s and early 1960s, guidance became part of pupil personnel services, with an emphasis on the counselor and counseling. This emphasis on position and process cast counselors primarily in a remedial-reactive role, and the pattern reinforced the practice of assigning administrative-clerical duties to counselors, since these duties fell under the broad catchall rubric of "service." Three organizational patterns for guidance prevailed, often in combination: the services model, the process model, and the duties model.

The *services model* had its origins in the 1920s; it consists of organizing the activities of counselors around six major services: (1) orientation, (2) assessment, (3) information, (4) counseling, (5) placement, and (6) followup. While the activities usually listed under each of these six services are important and useful, it is a limited model for three reasons. First, it is primarily oriented to secondary schools. Second, it does not lend itself easily to the identification of student outcomes. And third, it does not specify how the time of counselors should be allocated.

The *process model* also had its origins in the 1920s. Until the 1960s, this model emphasized the clinical and therapeutic aspects of counseling, particularly the processes that school counselors use: counseling, consulting, and coordinating. This model is appealing because it is equally applicable to elementary and secondary counselors. However, the process model has some of the same limitations as the services model: it does not lend itself easily to the identification of student outcomes and it does not specify allocations of counselor time.

Often, instead of describing some organizational pattern such as the services model or the process model, counselor duties are simply listed (the *duties model*). Sometimes these lists contain as many as 20 to 30 duties, and the last duty listed is often "and perform other duties as assigned from time to time." While the duties model is equally applied to elementary and secondary counselors, student outcomes are difficult to identify and counselor time is almost impossible to allocate effectively.

One result of these traditional organizational patterns was to emphasize the *position* of the counselor instead of the *program* of guidance. As a consequence, guidance became an ancillary-supportive service in the eyes of many people, an "add-on profession" that was marginal to the educational process. Furthermore, because of the absence of any clear structure to guidance programs, it was easy to give counselors new duties, since they were perceived as having free time and flexible schedules.

11

Accordingly, during the late 1960s and early 1970s, the concept of guidance for development emerged. During this period, the call came to reorient guidance from what had been an ancillary, crisis-oriented set of services to a comprehensive, developmental program. The call for reorientation came from diverse sources, including a renewed interest in vocational-career guidance (and its theoretical base, career development); concern about the efficacy of the prevailing approach to guidance in the schools; and concern about accountability and evaluation.

## The Comprehensive Guidance Program Model

In 1971, the University of Missouri-Columbia was awarded a U.S. Office of Education grant to assist each state, the District of Columbia, and Puerto Rico in developing models or guides for implementing career guidance, counseling, and placement programs in local schools. Pursuant to this grant, Gysbers and associates developed the first draft of the Comprehensive Guidance Model, an innovative organizational plan that sorted the activities of school counselors into three interrelated categories: curriculum-based functions, individual facilitation functions, and on-call functions (Gysbers 1990).

The *curriculum-based category* brought together those guidance activities that took place primarily in the context of regularly scheduled courses of study in an educational setting. These activities were a part of regular school subjects or were organized around special topics in the form of units, minicourses, or modules. They were based on need statements and goals and objectives necessary for the growth and development of all students. Topics often focused on self-understanding, interpersonal relationships, decision making, values clarification, and the education, work, and leisure worlds. School counselors were involved directly with students through class instruction, group processes, or individual discussion. In other instances, the guidance staff worked directly and cooperatively with teachers providing resources and consultation.

12

*Individual facilitation functions* included those systematic activities of the comprehensive guidance program designed to assist students in monitoring and understanding their growth and development in relation to their personal goals, values, abilities, aptitudes, and interests. School counselors and teachers served as "advisors," "learner managers," or "development specialists." Personalized contact and involvement were stressed instead of superficial contact with each student once a year to fill out a schedule. The functions in this category provided for the accountability needed in an educational setting to ensure that students' uniqueness remained intact and that educational resources were used to facilitate their life career development.

*On-call functions* focused on direct, immediate responses to students' needs such as information seeking, crisis counseling, and teacher/parent/specialist consultation. In addition, on-call functions supported the curriculum-based and individual facilitation functions. Adjunct guidance staff (peers, paraprofessionals, and volunteers/support staff) aided school counselors and teachers in carrying out on-call functions. Peers were involved in tutorial programs, orientation activities, ombudsman centers, and (with special training) cross-age counseling and leadership in informal dialogue centers. Paraprofessionals and volunteers provided meaningful services in placement and followup activities, community liaison, career information centers, and club leadership activities.

The 1974 version of the Model also used time distribution wheels to show the projected division of counselors' time to carry out a developmental guidance program. In addition, a chart was provided to show how counselors' time could be distributed across a typical school week using the three categories as organizers. In this arrangement, consultation as a process was added to the Model. By 1978, the focus was on a total comprehensive, developmental guidance program including the following elements: *Definition, Rationale, Assumptions, Content Model, and Process Model.* The *Content Model* described the knowledge and skills students would acquire with the guidance program; the *Process Model* grouped the guidance activities and processes used in the program into four interrelated categories: curriculum-based processes, individual-development processes, on-call responsive processes, and systems-support processes. Also in 1978, Gysbers described seven steps required to "remodel a guidance program while living in it" and to plan, implement, and evaluate a comprehensive guidance program (Gysbers 1990). These steps are as follows:

- Decide you want to change.

- Form work groups.

- Assess current programs.

- Select program model.

- Compare current program with program model.

- Establish transition timetable.

- Evaluate.

During the intervening years, this basic model has been adopted by school districts throughout the nation, and as a consequence of this extensive field testing, Gysbers has further developed and refined it. His most recent book, *Comprehensive Guidance Programs That Work* (Gysbers 1990) outlines the essential components of the current field-tested model and provides case histories of the implementation of this highly successful model in school districts throughout the nation.

## PROGRAM FOUNDATION

The perspective of human growth and development that serves as the foundation for the Model and as a basis for identifying the guidance knowledge, skills, and attitudes (competencies) that students need is called *Life Career Development*. This is defined as self-development over a person's life span through the integration of life roles, settings, and events. The word *life* indicates that the focus of this conception of human growth and development is on the total person—the human career. The word *career* in this context differs substantially from the usual definition of the term, in that it focuses on more than just an occupation; rather, it identifies the many and often varied roles that individuals assume (student, worker, consumer, citizen, parent); the settings in which individuals find themselves (home, school, community); and the events that occur over their lifetimes (entry job, marriage, divorce, retirement). It thus refers to all aspects of life, including physical, emotional, and intellectual development, personal relationships, responsibilities, and changing circumstances as interrelated parts of the whole person. Finally, the word *development* indicates that individuals are always in the process of becoming. When used in sequence, the words "life career development" bring these separate meanings together, but at the same time a greater meaning evolves. *Life Career Development* thus describes total, unique individuals with their own lifestyles; it is an organizing and integrating concept for understanding and facilitating human growth and development.

Wolfe and Kolb (1980) summed up the life view of career development:

> Career development involves one's whole life, not just occupation. As such, it concerns the whole person, needs and wants, capacities and potentials, excitements and anxieties, insights and blind spots, warts and all. More than that, it concerns him/her in the ever-changing contexts of his/her life. The environmental pressures and constraints, the bonds that tie him/her to significant others, responsibilities to children and aging parents, the total structure of one's circumstances are also factors that must be understood and reckoned with. In these terms, career development and personal development converge. Self and circumstances—evolving, changing, unfolding in mutual interaction—constitute the focus and the drama of career development. (pp. 1–2)

15

# PROGRAM CONTENT:
# LIFE CAREER DEVELOPMENT DOMAINS

Accordingly, the Model emphasizes three domains of human growth and development: (1) self-knowledge and interpersonal skills; (2) life roles, settings, and events; and (3) life career planning. Student competencies are derived from these domains to provide the program content for the Model. *Self-knowledge and interpersonal skills* focuses on helping students to develop awareness and acceptance of themselves and others, to create and maintain relationships, and to develop personal standards and a sense of purpose in life, which can then be used as a basis for life career planning. Students learn techniques for self-appraisal and the analysis of their personal characteristics, and they begin to formulate plans for self-improvement in such areas as physical and mental health. Individuals become knowledgeable about the interactive relationship between self and environment, so that they develop personal standards and a sense of purpose in life. They can use self-knowledge in career planning.

The second domain, *life roles, settings, and events,* emphasizes the interrelatedness of various life roles (such as learner, citizen, consumer), settings (such as home, school, work, and community), and events (such as job entry, marriage, and retirement) in which students participate over the life span. It emphasizes knowledge and understanding of the sociological, psychological, and economic dimensions and structure of their world. As students explore the different aspects of their roles, they learn how stereotypes affect their own and others' lives. They learn of the potential effects of change in modern society and of the necessity of being able to project themselves into the future. In this way, they begin to predict the future, foresee alternatives, and plan to meet the requirements of life career alternatives they may choose. As a result of learning about the multiple dimensions of their world, students understand the reciprocal influences of life roles, settings, and events, and can consider various lifestyle patterns.

The *life career planning* domain is designed to help students understand the importance of decision making and planning in everyday life and to appraise personal values as they relate to prospective life career plans and decisions. Students learn of the many occupations and industries in the work world and of their grouping according to occupational requirements and characteristics, as well as personal skills, interests, values, and aspirations. The central focus of this domain is on the mastery of decision-making skills as a part of life career planning. Students develop skills in gathering information from relevant sources, both external and internal, and in using the collected information to make informed and reasoned decisions. A major aspect of this process involves the appraisal of personal values as they may relate to prospective plans and decisions.

## PROGRAM STRUCTURE AND PROCESSES

The traditional model delineates six services (orientation, information, assessment, counseling, placement, and followup) and three aspects (educational, personal-social, and vocational) of school guidance. This "services" model of counseling results in an ancillary role for counseling, supportive of instruction rather than equal and complementary, while the "three aspects" view has led to fragmented and event-oriented activities.

In place of this traditional model, the *Comprehensive Guidance Program Model (CGPM)* consists of three structural foundations and four interactive program components. The *structural components*—definition, rationale, and assumptions— emphasize the centrality of guidance to the total education program, and define the relationship between guidance and other aspects of the curriculum. The *program components*—guidance curriculum, individual planning, responsive services, and system support—delineate the major activities, and the roles and responsibilities of personnel involved in the guidance program.

## Structural Components

The *program definition* includes the mission statement of the guidance program and emphasizes its centrality within the school district's total educational program. The *rationale* is directed at justifying the need for the competencies that will accrue to students as a result of their involvement in a comprehensive guidance program. It emphasizes the importance of guidance as an equal partner in the education system and draws conclusions from student and community needs assessments and clarifications of goals for the local educational system. The *assumptions* are the principles that shape and guide the program, including statements on the contribution that school counselors and guidance programs make to students' development, the premises that undergird the comprehensiveness and balanced nature of the program, and the relationship between the guidance program and other educational programs.

## Program Components

The four program components delineate the major activities, and the roles and responsibilities of personnel involved in the guidance program. The concept of a *guidance curriculum* is at the core of the model; it is based on the assumption that guidance programs should provide knowledge and skills in the three domains—self-knowledge, life roles, and life career planning—that all students can learn in a systematic, sequential way. The guidance curriculum typically consists of *structured classroom activities,* organized around the three domains of student competencies—self-knowledge and interpersonal skills; life roles, settings, and events; and life career planning. Counselors and teachers collaborate in teaching guidance curriculum units and activities in the classroom, guidance center, or other school facilities. Counselors also organize and conduct *large group activities* such as career days and educational/college/vocational days. Although counselors' responsibilities include organizing and implementing the guidance curriculum, the cooperation and support of the entire faculty are necessary for its success. For this reason, counselor-teacher cooperation is essential.

The *individual planning* component of the Model consists of activities and procedures to assist students in understanding their goals, values, abilities, aptitudes, and interests and periodically monitoring their growth and development. These activities help students to plan, monitor, and manage their own learning and their personal and career development. The focus is on helping students to develop, analyze, and evaluate their educational, occupational, and personal goals and plans. Individual planning is implemented through such activities as the following:

- *individual appraisal,* through which counselors assist students in assessing and interpreting their abilities, interests, skills, and achievement;

- *individual assessment,* through which counselors assist students in using self-appraisal information along with personal-social, educational, career, and labor market information to help them plan for and realize their personal, educational, and occupational goals;

- *placement,* through which counselors assist students in making the transition from school to work or to additional education and training.

The *responsive services* component consists of guidance techniques to meet immediate personal problems. Through this component, counselors address problems related to academic learning, personal identity issues, drugs, and peer and family relationships, as well as crisis counseling, diagnostic and remediation activities, and consultation and referral. In addition, a guidance program needs to respond to the immediate information-seeking needs of students, parents, and teachers.

Responsive services are implemented through strategies such as the following:

- *consultation* with parents, teachers, other educators, and community agencies to help students resolve personal concerns;

- *personal counseling,* individually or in small groups, to help students deal with relationships, personal concerns, and development, and to help them identify problems and causes, alternatives, and possible consequences;

- *crisis counseling* and support for students or their families facing emergency situations; and

- *referral* to other professional resources such as mental health agencies, employment and training programs, social services, or special education programs.

The responsive services component also provides intensive small group counseling for students with similar concerns. Adjunct guidance staff—peers, paraprofessionals, and volunteers—can aid counselors in carrying out responsive services, while peers can be involved in tutorial programs, orientation activities, ombudsman functions, and—with special training—cross-age counseling and leadership in informal dialogue. Paraprofessionals and volunteers can provide assistance in such areas as placement, followup, and community-school-home liaison activities.

Finally, the management of a comprehensive guidance program requires ongoing *system support.* This component consists of management activities that establish, maintain, and enhance the total guidance program. It is carried out through the following activities:

- *research and development*—including guidance program evaluation, followup studies, and the continued development and updating of guidance learning activities;

- *staff/community public relations*—through newsletters, local media, and school and community presentations;

- *professional development*—activities such as school in-service training, attendance at professional meetings, completion of postgraduate coursework, and contributions to professional literature;

- *committee/advisory boards*—such as service on curriculum committees, or ad hoc school-community commissions;

- *community outreach*—activities to help counselors become knowledgeable about community resources, employment opportunities, social service agencies, and the local labor market; and

- *program management and operations*—the planning and management tasks needed to support the activities of a comprehensive guidance program.

Also included in this component are activities that support programs other than guidance, such as interpreting the results of a school testing program, serving on departmental curriculum committees, and working with school administrators. Counselors must carefully monitor the time they spend on system support, however, because their prime focus should be on implementing the *guidance curriculum,* assisting with *individual planning,* and *responsive services.* If a guidance program is run well, focusing on these three components, it will provide substantial support for other programs and personnel in the school and the community.

## PROGRAM TIME AND RESOURCES

One principal rationale behind the Comprehensive

21

Guidance Program Model is to enable counselors to regain control of their time on the job. The four program components discussed above are thus intended to provide the structure for making judgments about appropriate allocations of counselors' time. The Model should therefore be considered a *100 percent program,* meaning that it should be understood from the outset that 100 percent of counselors' time must be spread across the four program components: guidance curriculum, individual planning, responsive services, and system support. Although time allocations can be adjusted, based on grade levels or on changing needs, nothing new can be added to implementing the guidance program. No more than *10 to 15 percent* of counselor time should be allocated to system support; the rest of the time should be divided among the guidance curriculum, individual planning, and responsive services, with a gradual shift in emphasis from guidance curriculum to individual planning as students grow older.

## Human Resources

While counselors are the main providers of guidance and counseling services and are the coordinators of the program, the success of the program also depends on the involvement, cooperation, and support of teachers, administrators, parents, community members, and business and labor personnel. For this reason, a school/community advisory committee should be formed to provide a human resource base for the program. The committee should act as a liaison between the school and community and provide recommendations concerning the needs of students and of the community. It is not, however, a policy or decision-making body; rather, its primary duty is to provide advice, counsel, and support for those involved in the guidance program, and to serve as a communication link between the guidance program, the school, and the community.

## Financial Resources and Facilities

The Model also describes the financial resources, including budget, materials, equipment, and facilities, needed to ensure the success of a comprehensive guidance program. The Model highlights the need for these resources through its focus on the physical space and equipment required to implement the program. Guidance facilities normally consist of a suite of offices designed primarily for one-on-one counseling, often with a waiting area where students can browse through displays of educational or occupational information. These offices have typically been located in the administrative wing of the school so that counseling staff could be near student records and the administration.

Although counselors still need individual offices in a comprehensive guidance program, they also need to open up guidance facilities to make them more accessible to all students, teachers, parents, and community members. A guidance center should therefore be created to bring together available guidance information and resources and to make them easily accessible to students. The center would be used for such activities as group sessions, self-exploration, and personalized research and planning. At the high school level, students could receive assistance in areas such as occupational planning, job entry and placement, financial aid information, and postsecondary educational opportunities. The elementary school guidance center could provide information to students and their parents about the school, the community, parenthood, and child development, as well as an area for play therapy.

However designed, the guidance center should be organized primarily for students, with many of the activities planned and directed by students. It could also be a valuable resource for teachers in planning their programs, and for potential employers in seeking part-time or full-time workers. Community members and parents should also be involved in the planning and implementation of the center and its activities.

The guidance center should be furnished as comfortably as possible for all users, with provisions for group as well as individual activities. The guidance staff coordinates its operation, but all school staff should be involved in planning, staffing, and using the center.

## SUMMARY

By definition, the Comprehensive Guidance Program Model leads to guidance activities and structured group experiences for all students. It deemphasizes administrative and clerical tasks, the ad hoc service-oriented approach, and limited accountability. Counselors spend 100 percent of their time implementing the guidance program; they have no leftover time for unrelated administrative and clerical duties. To fully implement the Model, the program should be:

- *student-development-oriented,* not oriented toward school maintenance or administration;

- *a 100 percent program,* in which the Comprehensive Guidance Program Model accounts for all of counselors' time, without add-ons;

- *started the first day and ended the last day of school,* not started in the middle of October with an ending time in April so that administrative, nonguidance tasks can be completed;

- *program-focused,* not position-focused; and

- *education-based,* not agency- or clinic-based.

Chapter 2

# THE TEACHER ADVISOR PROGRAM

by **Robert D. Myrick,** Professor of Counselor Education, School of Education, University of Florida, Gainesville; and **Linda S. Myrick,** Educational Consultant

*The assumption behind the Myricks' Teacher Advisor Program model (TAP) is that each student needs a friendly adult in the school who knows and cares about him or her in a personal way. The advisors help their advisees deal with the problems of growing up and getting the most out of school. A teacher-advisor is usually responsible for an advisee's cumulative folder, work folders, teacher-student conferences, parent conferences, group guidance experiences, and followup on academic progress reports. Advisors also consult with other teachers, school counselors, and support personnel about their advisees.*

## OVERVIEW

Every successful counseling and guidance intervention used in schools is aimed at developing a young person's potential; this depends on mobilizing untapped resources. Although many students are doing quite well and enjoy school, a great number of the nation's youth feel alienated from school and society. These students often begin school on a rough and uncertain path that is likely to lead them to dependent, unproductive lives. These are high-risk students, and they are found in every school district.

### Students at Risk

High-risk students fall into various categories: school dropouts, chronic truants, underachievers, economically disad-

25

vantaged, non-English speakers, substance abusers, aggressive delinquents, pregnant teenagers, migrants, physically abused and neglected, and learning disabled. While they may be different in age, sex, or race, live in different communities, attend different schools, and have different teachers, they share a few things in common—all live under difficult social circumstances, have problems with school, and struggle with the learning process. The school environment is often unresponsive to them. We need to assist such children in their transition to adulthood. Likewise, we need to help our nation, as it too is in transition and at risk:

- One in five children lives below the poverty level. America's childhood-poverty rate is *two to three times higher* than that of most other industrialized nations, which offer more generous benefits for the poor.

- One in five children lives with one parent, and half of these parents are poor. The number of female heads of household has doubled since 1970 and tripled since 1960. One-third of such women live below the poverty level.

- The teenage pregnancy rate in the United States is the *highest of 30 developed nations* and has increased 12 percent since 1973. Fifty percent of these girls fail to complete school and earn less than half the income of those who wait to start their families.

- The average public high school today loses *25 percent* of its potential graduates. The range of dropouts for states is 11 to 44 percent.

- There is a high rate of youth unemployment and a greater threat of prolonged periods of unemployment and low earnings among Black and Hispanic groups.

- By the end of the ninth grade, about 30 percent of all students have experimented with illegal drugs. Before graduating from high school, 90 percent have experi-

26

mented with alcohol, some use cocaine, and many have become dependent on stimulants.

These and other statistics provide a picture of what it is like for many growing up in America. They highlight changing populations and the daily challenges that face teachers and other educators.

## The Need for Reform

In order that the United States may become more competitive in the global marketplace, many of our nation's leaders are calling for a complete restructuring of the schools. Many of the restructuring proposals are familiar to us: more peer helping, tutoring, smaller classes, small study groups, cooperative learning, self-instruction workbooks, computers and lab equipment, and new or revised curricula. Other suggested changes are more profound and include the way teachers perceive and work with students. For example, the needs and interests of students must be given more consideration and there must be more shared responsibility for helping students learn. More teamwork may be the most essential, realistic, and practical reform available to all schools.

In our high-tech information society, we can no longer prepare students for industrial jobs that demand specific knowledge and conformity. While assembly-line teaching methods are still the norm in many schools, assembly-line jobs are decreasing and are now almost a part of the past. Moreover, we can no longer prepare students as if they were going to live in an unchanging community, unaffected by a global economy, ecological deterioration, or a nation's social unrest. We cannot continue to have a semiliterate work force that has trouble adjusting to change and communicating with others.

Teachers, especially in the secondary schools, have been encouraged for several decades to be specialists in their respective subject areas, sometimes at the expense of being team players.

Too many teachers have drifted into relying on a set curriculum, rather than tailoring it to meet the needs and interests of students. Furthermore, the report by the task force of the Carnegie Council on Adolescent Development (1989) emphasized that the middle grades have been virtually ignored in the school reform debates; as a consequence, "Most young adolescents attend massive, impersonal schools, learn from unconnected curricula, know well and trust few adults in school, and lack access to health care and counseling" (p. 13). Far too many young people feel lost and are vulnerable; an already difficult period of their lives is often made more so by the nature of our schools.

*Approaches to Guidance for Students at Risk*

When a crisis is at hand, attention is immediately focused on the situation and treatment. On occasion, this crisis approach to guidance cannot be avoided, but it is questionable in terms of long-term effectiveness. At several conferences on education in 1988, various task forces claimed that an early investment in children could do much to prevent crime, poor health, unemployment, and social ills. They proposed comprehensive and timely prenatal care, health care for young children to prevent diseases and disabilities, and accessible and affordable day care. This preventive approach makes more sense than waiting to react with more costly solutions. The recommendations of the National Governors' Association Task Force on Children (1989) included the following:

- developing a tracking system for high-risk students;
- reorganizing large middle schools into smaller, more manageable units, so that young people can gain independence while remaining in a more intimate environment;
- encouraging schools to create youth-service programs within their curricula;
- providing more support for families and their children.

In the 1980s, more than 1,000 pieces of proposed state legislation related to education and teacher policies. Only a fraction were approved and implemented. Very often, these bills did not reflect a consensus of opinion and they lacked specific guidelines and funding. Mandating competency-based tests, attendance and course requirements, more graduation credits, or merit pay for outstanding teachers have not proven to be valid solutions.

## The Developmental Approach

Despite the eagerness to solve problems and to improve education, we sometimes lose sight of the most viable concept for helping young people: the developmental approach. This approach recognizes that each individual is unique but progresses through some common growth stages with related needs. It identifies time periods in life when people typically experience extensive changes in their physiological and biochemical systems, which in turn affect their thinking and behavior. Attitudes, habits, and skill development are related to certain stages of development and, if attended to in a positive way, can provide the foundation for future success. As a starting point, consider the following as criteria to test whether or not schools and educational programs are developmentally appropriate:

- attention to individual differences in student growth patterns and rates of growth;

- focus on all aspects of development: physical, social, emotional, cognitive and personal;

- integrated curriculum rather than isolated skill development;

- active rather than passive learning;

- concrete, hands-on learning materials;

- small group instruction;

29

- multicultural and nonsexist curriculum;

- peer interaction and group problem solving;

- heterogeneous grouping of students;

- flexible strategies for involving students in the learning process;

- opportunities for decision making and problem solving.

Although crisis and prevention strategies will always receive special attention by reformers in education, the approach that incorporates both and that makes the most sense is the developmental approach.

## Teachers and Developmental Guidance

If counselors are to meet the urgent needs of young people in our rapidly changing society, they will need the cooperation and support of the rest of the educational staff, and especially of those who have the greatest amount of contact with students: the teachers.

Teachers are no strangers to guidance; prior to the 1960s, most books about school guidance were directed to them. Since there were few guidance specialists, teachers were commonly assumed to be responsible for helping the child grow personally and socially, as well as academically. It is only more recently, as schools have become larger and teachers have taken on greater numbers of students, that guidance has been relegated to specialists.

The first wave of high school counselors, who appeared in 1957 after Sputnik was launched by the Soviet Union, spent most of their time on testing and identifying students who might be encouraged to attend college and become national assets as mathematicians, engineers, or scientists. In a short time, these counselors were asked to go beyond college placement and help with the vocational needs of adolescents. They were also expected

30

to counsel students who had special problems, particularly with school adjustment.

Because of the high counselor-student ratio—normally ranging from 1:200 to 1:500—many troubled students have fallen between the cracks and have been unable to receive help. Frustrated teachers continue to refer these students for assistance, believing that the counselor has more time, is more skilled, and is more likely to be effective. Ironically, many counselors are minimally prepared, are overloaded with referrals, and have little access to students without disrupting their academic schedules. It is clear that counselors, or other specialists, cannot accept total responsibility for guidance and counseling. Good teaching is, and always will be, the heart of good school guidance.

## THE TEACHER ADVISOR PROGRAM (TAP)

One of the most innovative ways to make sure that all students benefit from developmental guidance and counseling is to directly involve teachers in Teacher Advisor Programs (TAP). Teachers are designated as advisors to groups of 18 to 25 students and meet with their advisees both individually and in group sessions. The basic assumption is that each student needs a friendly adult in the school who knows and cares about the student in a personal way.

When students have problems, they turn to those who they know are available to them and who they think can offer them the most help. Surveys show that elementary students turn first to their parents and then to their teachers. The majority of adolescents turn first to peers and then to relatives and teachers. In general, students choose their first line of helpers from among those people whom they see almost every day, especially if they have positive relationships with them.

Surprisingly, school counselors and other support personnel, who are professionally trained in helping people with personal problems, are not typically the student's first choice of helper. First, counselors often lack the visibility of teachers or peers. Second, a school counselor's image may be aligned with authority, discipline, and administrative procedures. While this is changing, counselors still do not have daily contact with most students and consequently may not be seen in general as "friendly advisors or helpers."

## Teachers as Advisors

Classroom teachers have a history of helping students who have personal problems. Some teachers continue to be a source of guidance to their students long after they have left their classes or the school. This is especially true when the teacher-student relationship has been personal and meaningful to both parties. If students perceive teachers as caring and interested in them, they are more likely to be inspired and enjoy going to school; they feel encouraged and try harder.

Research shows that effective teachers have the same perceived characteristics as effective guidance and counseling specialists. Among these characteristics are the willingness and ability to

- see the student's point of view;

- personalize the education experience;

- facilitate a class discussion where students listen and share ideas;

- develop a helping relationship with students and parents;

- organize personal learning experiences;

- be flexible;

- be open to trying new ideas;

- model interpersonal and communication skills;

- foster a positive learning environment.

Elementary school teachers have traditionally accepted their roles as guidance teachers. They work in self-contained classrooms and have many opportunities to be aware of the needs and interests of students, to build close relationships, and to provide timely developmental guidance. Secondary school teachers, however, work with larger numbers of students and spend limited amounts of time with them. It is not uncommon for many of the core curriculum teachers in junior and senior high schools to have six classes, with as many as 30 or more students in each class. Thus, a teacher may meet with more than 180 students a day, seeing them for less than an hour in class. Therefore it is not surprising that so few secondary school students enjoy the luxury of close working relationships with their teachers.

Popular and assertive students are usually able to establish enduring and helpful relationships with their teachers. Yet many other students who need adult guidance and a mature relationship that they can draw upon are too shy or withdrawn to reach out to teachers for help. And some students are aware that their attitudes and behaviors in school are not what is expected and that teachers are not likely to be interested in them.

Teacher Advisor Programs can therefore meet the need for teachers to be directly involved in developmental guidance at all levels. The advisors help their advisees deal with the problems of growing up and getting the most out of school. TAP is thus a valid developmental guidance approach that can help young people realize more of their potential as well as strengthen our nation's human resources.

### Origins of TAP in the Middle Schools

The teacher advisor program was first described as a "homebase" or "homeroom" for students when it was introduced into the middle schools during the 1960s. The assumption was that young adolescents faced certain stresses related to their physical and social development that, in turn, affected their educational progress. It was called the age of transience, a time of more choices and decisions, more personal and social responsibilities, and more academic expectations, leading to a greater variance in student achievement and progress.

The term "affective education" was popular when middle school teacher advisement programs started in the 1960s and was used to build a rationale for advisor-advisee programs. But the general public was suspicious about activities that focused on nonacademic aspects of education such as self-concept, values clarification, self-disclosure, and moral and social development. Lacking an adequate understanding of developmental guidance and its relation to helping students learn more effectively and efficiently, most educators were skeptical and failed to systematically develop teacher-based guidance. Advisor-advisee programs, as they were also called then, met with limited success because they were poorly defined, teacher preparation was minimal, and apprehension prevailed among teachers, counselors, and administrators. Nonetheless, a recent study of middle schools by Alexander and McEwin (1989) showed that 77 percent of 181 middle schools scheduled advisory periods five times a week.

## High School Teacher Advisor Programs

Transition does not stop at the middle school. For this reason, developmental guidance and the need for students to have an adult advisor also appealed to some high school faculties. For example, Wilde Lake High School in Columbia, Maryland, took the position that guidance was everyone's responsibility. Each teacher worked with 20 to 25 students in multi-aged groups and was charged with becoming a "significant other" to his or her advisees. As a consequence, counselors were freed to work with students with special needs who were referred to them (Jenkins 1977).

## Who Should Be Advisors for Whom?

In a well-designed Teacher Advisor Program, all teachers

and most available staff should be assigned advisory groups. This allows for a reasonable advisor-advisee ratio and for all staff to share equal responsibility for advisement in the school, although local conditions, constraints, and policies may influence the designation of advisors.

Many students select their advisors by indicating choices at the time of registration. Other schools follow random procedures, giving special attention to balancing groups by gender, race, academic ability, and general performance in school. It is wise to make sure that no advisor is overloaded with students with serious problems.

Some schools insist that, once assigned, an advisor and an advisory group work together as long as the students remain at the school. It is assumed that such continuity enables the group and the advisor to build greater trust and to know each other better. Other schools reassign students to advisors and advisory groups at the beginning of each school year, hoping that students will get to know more than just one group of peers and one adult who has taken the time to know them.

It might make sense to group students with special interests, but keeping all exceptional education students together is not necessarily a good idea. These students need to be mainstreamed in developmental guidance. Likewise, keeping all band students or those interested in a particular career goal together may also be defeating in the long run. Students need a heterogeneous group of peers in their advisory groups.

Some schools have reduced the number of students assigned to each advisor by assigning groups to all but one of their counselors. These groups often consist of those who want to be "peer facilitators" or "peer counselors." Thus, with the assistance of the counselors, these students learn how to help others in the first few weeks of school and then work as peer facilitators.

## Responsibilities

In addition to their academic classes, teachers are

assigned a group of about 20 students. There may be more or less, depending on the number of students and participating faculty, but the best ratio appears to be about 1:15. A teacher-advisor is usually responsible for an advisee's cumulative folder, work folders, teacher-student conferences, parent conferences, group guidance experiences, and followup on academic progress reports. Advisors also consult with other teachers, school counselors, and support personnel about their advisees.

TAP is designed to provide an opportunity for all the students in a school to participate in a small and cohesive group of 15 to 25 peers led by a sensitive and caring teacher who promotes and monitors individual students' educational and developmental experiences as they progress through school. Teacher-advisors meet with their advisees on a regular basis through a "homeroom" or "homebase" group.

This homeroom becomes, in effect, the students' home within the school, where they have a supportive teacher and group of peers with whom they can explore personal interests, goals, and concerns. A guidance curriculum is usually part of TAP; it is presented during advisory meetings, which range from 25 to 30 minutes in length at the beginning of each school day. At least two days of the week are scheduled for developmental guidance activities. The other three days are more flexible and might be used for supervised study, tutoring, journal writing, silent reading, minicourses, clubs, exploration of music and the arts, or for more guidance activities.

Some schools have scheduled homebase meetings in other ways. Scheduling meetings every school day is ideal, since it gives advisors and advisees more opportunities to know each other. It also gives a faculty and staff more opportunities to be creative with those days that are not allotted for group guidance activities.

In any case, it appears that the homebase period should be no less than 25 minutes if a guidance curriculum is to be delivered with any degree of effectiveness. That amount of time is needed to guide students through most structured activities.

Time must be managed very carefully, and the sessions should be task-oriented, since advisors tend to rush, lose patience, and give up on group activities when time is short.

## Advisor Skills and Preparation

Teachers need special preparation in how to work with their students in guidance sessions and how to build guidance units for their groups. Some sessions are more structured than others. Some are designed to build group cohesiveness and a sense of belonging among advisees in their homebase period. Others attempt to anticipate the developmental needs of students, while still other sessions depend upon what students want to talk about and the particular needs and interests that emerge.

One teacher-advisor argued that students didn't like or benefit from a study skills unit that had been delivered during homeroom guidance. However, further examination showed that he was depending exclusively upon printed materials and was telling students how to study. This teacher missed the point of guidance, he was working too hard, and he was denying students an opportunity to learn from each other. He was encouraged by a TAP coordinator to put aside the printed materials and encourage the group members to talk about study habits from their own experiences. This approach makes the topic more personally meaningful and more interesting.

## Guidance Curriculum

The guidance curriculum varies from one school to another, but it generally addresses personal, social, and academic concerns. Some of the personal and social skills addressed include getting acquainted, self-esteem, time management, conflict management, and classroom behavior. Academic topics might include policies and procedures from the school handbook, computing grade point averages, finding meaning in test results, developing study skills and habits, standardized tests and test anxiety, and learning styles. A few career and educational planning topics include career exploration and choices, employability skills, the job market, what employers look for, alternative jobs in career fields, job applications, resume writing, and community services.

Each developmental guidance unit focuses on a particular topic, such as getting acquainted, study skills and habits, self-assessment, communication skills, decision making and problem solving, peer relationships, conflict resolution, or career development. Other units may be developed in light of special student needs or interests. Each three-week unit is organized around a general scheme of six sessions, five of which consist of guidance activities and a final one that is reserved for evaluation of the unit. Some units are designed to build group cohesiveness, while others anticipate the students' developmental needs; still others depend on what students themselves want to talk about. A well-designed guidance curriculum might include the following kinds of units:

- *Getting Acquainted*—a unit to help TAP group members get to know each other, learn to participate, and review school procedures.

- *Study Skills and Habits*—a unit focusing on such topics as time management, classroom listening skills, test-taking skills, and grades.

- *Self-Assessment*—a unit to help students identify and evaluate their classroom behavior and performance; to assess personal attitudes about school, self, teacher and others; to identify interests and abilities; and to set goals and monitor progress.

- *Communication Skills*—a unit focusing on facilitative interpersonal skills such as listening, sensitivity, and thoughtful participation, and assessing effects of one's behavior on others.

- *Decision Making and Problem Solving*—a unit focusing on skills involved in identifying alternatives and consequences and making wise and timely decisions when confronted by common teenage dilemmas.

- *Peer Relationships*—a unit for examining sex roles and sex stereotypes, as well as for developing positive ways to interact with peers, to develop friendships, to become aware of how personal needs and interests affect relationships, and to resist undesirable peer pressure.

- *Motivation*—a unit focusing on becoming aware of interests, needs, and desires, and on the link between self-esteem and approaches to achieving personally meaningful goals.

- *Conflict/Resolution*—a unit whose purpose is to identify how and when conflict can occur and to learn constructive ways of dealing with it.

- *Wellness*—a unit whose purpose is to discuss how exercise, nutrition, positive attitudes, and personal living habits can affect students' lives, to examine the long-range consequences of alcohol and drug abuse, and to develop effective ways of coping with stress.

- *Career Development*—a unit focusing on jobs, occupations, and careers, and how these are related to interests, needs, skills, opportunities, and goals.

- *Educational Planning*—a unit focusing on the need to plan academic courses, requirements, and electives for middle or high school.

- *Community Involvement*—a unit aimed at developing a sense of responsibility as citizens in the community, and identifying opportunities to volunteer for community service.

# COUNSELORS AND TEACHER ADVISORS

Many high school teachers have never had a guidance course and many are unsure of how to lead a group discussion with adolescents when no lesson is to be taught. It is difficult for them to put aside old teacher modes and habits and to become better listeners and facilitators. Many are uncertain as to how to use TAP time and far too many do not understand the basic principles of developmental guidance and TAP. Consequently, it is not uncommon for a beginning teacher advisor program to meet initially with teacher skepticism, apprehension, and resistance.

To become better listeners and facilitators, teachers may therefore need special preparation in how to work with their students in guidance sessions and how to build guidance units for their groups. Some sessions are more structured than others; some are designed to build group cohesiveness and a sense of belonging among advisees; others attempt to anticipate the developmental needs of students; and still others depend on the particular needs and interests of the students.

Counselors can therefore assist teachers in developing guidance units, or they can work together as a team in developing and delivering a guidance curriculum, with counselors taking over homebase groups on occasion. It is important, therefore, to establish a cooperative and supportive relationship between teachers and counselors so that they can define their respective roles and differentiate responsibilities. Counselors can assist teachers in the following ways:

- *Co-lead some guidance units* and sessions with teachers, when appropriate.

- *Work with teachers* who are having trouble managing their groups.

- *Develop special guidance units* based on the needs of a particular student population, or in specific contexts.

- *Meet for small group counseling* with selected student groups that are disruptive, or that may have special problems adjusting, or that may have special needs and interests, during TAP period.

- *Meet for individual counseling* with disruptive students, or others referred by the teacher during TAP period.

- *Serve as consultants* and personal resources to teachers about TAP. If a full- or part-time TAP coordinator is not employed in a school, it is common for a school counselor to assume leadership and coordinate TAP, often with a teacher as co-leader or through a steering committee.

- *Organize a peer facilitator training program* to train students in such roles as teacher-assistant, tutor, special friend, or small group leader. Teacher-advisors can then draw upon these students to help them lead group discussions in their advisory groups or to help their advisees individually.

## BUILDING SUPPORT FOR TAP

Despite the apparent value of TAP, many middle/junior and high school teachers are reluctant to support it. In general, about 20 percent of most secondary school faculties will quickly embrace the program. These teachers like the idea of developmental guidance and they have the skills and personality to put the program in practice without much preparation, since they thoroughly enjoy the opportunity to form closer helping relationships with students.

Another 20 percent of a school faculty, in general, are clearly resistant. They argue against it and see only an extra preparation for themselves. To them TAP is a waste of time. They erroneously believe that guidance should be left to specialists, such as counselors and school psychologists. Many are uncertain about how to use TAP time, or they do not understand the basic principles of developmental guidance. They see it only as an extra burden on their time, and they believe that guidance should be left to specialists. This reluctant group of teachers needs special assistance or in-service training if they are to become supportive and involved in building a program. Unfortunately, of this 20 percent, probably half of them may not have the personality, skills, interests, or energy to make TAP work and they may need to be assigned other duties.

The middle 60 percent of the faculty makes the critical difference. If this group is for TAP, then the program will make a positive contribution in the school. If the majority of teachers are against TAP, then the program will have trouble surviving; it will be sabotaged, and thus will be a tremendous waste of time and energy.

To enlist the support of a school's faculty for TAP and developmental guidance, the following factors are critical:

- *Understand the philosophy of TAP.* This includes an understanding of student needs and an awareness of student problems. It also includes a recognition of how guidance is related to helping students learn more effectively, as well as to helping them grow socially and personally.

- *Commit adequate time for TAP.* Some teacher advisor programs suffer because there is not enough time for advisors to meet with their advisees. There is little chance that caring and helping relationships will develop if meeting times are limited, sporadic, or lacking in continuity. Twice a week is the minimum; every day would be ideal, to give advisors an opportunity to know their students and get involved in the program.

- *Provide a developmental guidance curriculum guide.* Teachers are used to having curriculum guides and they often depend on learning activities to stimulate student thinking and participation. Teachers like to have organized guidance handbooks that contain various activities that they might use in TAP. The curriculum guide should establish guidance objectives and provide activities, but allow teachers to choose or discard suggested activities according to their needs.

- *Prepare teachers in guidance and interpersonal skills.* Since most teachers have not had a course in guidance, many do not know how a guidance program is developed to meet student needs and how guidance interventions can be used to help students. Teachers may have limited conferring skills and many are unsure of how to manage groups in an open discussion. More specifically, far too many teachers rely on one group arrangement—all students facing the front of the room—and need more training in how to get students working cooperatively in small groups. Many teachers also need to know how to help students think about a personal problem and to take some steps in solving a problem. The basic skills that teachers need include responding to students' feelings, clarifying or summarizing ideas, asking open-ended questions, complimenting and confronting, linking feelings and ideas, setting limits, and acknowledging contributions.

- *Have visible administrative support.* Administrators set the tone of a school through their personal styles and commitment, so the success of a TAP program requires their visible and active support. If administrators are supportive, then teachers will try harder. If they are indifferent, then teachers will find other places to invest their time and energy. Administrators can increase their visibility in the schools by visiting TAP groups and talking with students when discipline is not an issue. They can talk with TAP coordinators about guidance units and, on occasion, they might co-lead or lead a discussion in one of the TAP homerooms.

- *Establish consistent procedures for evaluating TAP.* Program evaluations provide data upon which to monitor the success of the program and make decisions about future modifications. It takes time to develop an excellent program: adjustments must be made, priorities must be set, and people must learn to work together. With feedback from students and teachers, it is possible to keep TAP moving in the desired direction.

Although the full support of counselors and administrators is essential, teachers are the heart of this developmental guidance program. They work directly with students in their classes and student-teacher relationships influence the school atmosphere. Counselors support teachers in their work, and they need the teachers' assistance if they are to fully understand a student's world. They also need cooperation from teachers if they are to have access to students for their own interventions. Only with teacher involvement and commitment, at all grade levels, is such a program possible.

Teachers and counselors must therefore work together as a team to provide the kind of comprehensive developmental guidance program that meets the urgent needs of today's students. Developmental guidance and counseling services are essential factors in the pursuit of educational excellence.

Chapter 3

# INVITATIONAL LEARNING FOR COUNSELING AND DEVELOPMENT

by **William W. Purkey,** Professor of Counselor Education, University of North Carolina, Greensboro; and **John J. Schmidt,** Associate Professor of Education and Acting Chair of Counselor and Adult Education, East Carolina University, Greenville, North Carolina

*The Invitational Learning concept, developed by William W. Purkey, is a new paradigm that seeks to redress the all-too-common forbidding school climate by reconstituting the entire school—people, places, policies, programs, and processes—so that every aspect serves to "invite" students to learn by respecting them, encouraging them, and validating their unique importance and possibilities. Invitational Learning thus provides all school staff with a plan for enriching the physical and psychological environments of schools and encouraging the development of the people who work in them.*

## OVERVIEW

Invitational Learning is a complex of facilitative psychological attitudes that takes a theoretical stance regarding the marvelous possibilities within each person and applies this stance in countless helping relationships designed to enrich existence and facilitate development. Simply stated, Invitational Learning offers a blueprint of what counselors, teachers, principals, supervisors, superintendents, and others can do to enrich the physical and psychological environments of institutions and to encourage the development of the people who work there.

Invitational Learning claims as its province the global nature of institutions, including people, places, policies, programs, and processes. These five "P's" in combination with other elements of Invitational Learning offer a paradigm for personal and professional functioning. Invitational Learning is based on four value-based assumptions regarding the nature of people and their potential and the nature of professional helping:

- *Respect:* People are able, valuable, and responsible and should be treated accordingly.

- *Trust:* Education should be a collaborative, cooperative activity where process is as important as product.

- *Optimism:* People possess untapped potential in all areas of human endeavor.

- *Intentionality:* Human potential can best be realized by places, policies, programs, and processes that are specifically designed to invite development, and by people who are intentionally inviting with themselves and others, personally and professionally.

These four assumptions will now be considered in detail.

## Respect

Respect for the uniqueness, value, and integrity of each human being is the cornerstone of the Invitational Learning approach. Only when we accept people as they are, recognize their unlimited potential for development, and invite them to assume responsibility for their lives and make appropriate, caring decisions regarding their present and future, do we contribute to their well-being. Developing respect in human relationships depends on an attitude manifested in a dependable and consistent pattern of action, and on considering at all times the needs and wishes of those whom we seek to serve.

Few relationships in life can be productive and helpful without respect for the integrity of the people involved. In professional counseling, for example, respect is sometimes fragile because clients are frequently at an ebb point in their lives. They are desperately looking toward others to be "rescued" or "saved." But such actions are in opposition to Invitational Learning. To deny the person's authority over his or her own life, to take away the person's ultimate responsibility for his or her own existence, is disrespectful. No matter how much we would like people to do what we wish them to do, no matter how beneficial the desired actions appear to be, and no matter how much the person wants us to take charge of his or her life, Invitational Learning is firm: each individual is responsible for his or her own life. People are able, valuable, and responsible and should be treated accordingly.

Respect also involves knowing when to invite and when not to invite, when to accept and when not to accept. Doing things for people that they should do for themselves, giving unsolicited advice, saying yes when we want to say no, are all examples of lack of respect. A respectful stance means that when we offer something beneficial for consideration, we accept the condition that the process of inviting is fluid, and that the needs and wishes of those whom we seek to serve are just as important as our own needs and wishes.

## Trust

Trust, the second vital quality in Invitational Learning, recognizes the interdependence of human beings and emphasizes that professional helping should be a collaborative, cooperative activity where process is as important as product. As John Dewey explained a half century ago, it is absurd to suppose that a person gets more intellectual or mental discipline when he or she goes at a matter unwillingly than when he or she goes at it out of fullness of heart. Trust is enhanced when we give high priority to optimal human welfare, when we view places, policies, programs, and processes as contributing to or subtracting from this welfare, and when we recognize that working for the benefit of everyone is the best way to ensure our own welfare.

Trust is seldom won by a single inviting act; rather, it depends on establishing an inviting pattern of actions, characterized by caring, purposeful, and active commitment, that establishes a mutually trustful relationship between counselors and clients or teachers and students. One difference between Invitational Learning and other approaches to professional helping is that some others require that a trustful relationship be established *before* any progress can be made. Invitational Learning, by contrast, begins with the desire to help, a willingness to "be with" others, a deliberate preparation of all conditions needed to establish trust, and a genuine response to the concerns of those involved. These attitudes, conditions, and characteristics set the stage for trust to develop.

The condition of establishing trust is observed most clearly when counselors work with clients who have violated the trust of others, or who have had their trust violated—for example, individuals who have committed crimes and are incarcerated, or individuals who have been abused by others. Building trust with such individuals is done over time as a result of the caring and dependable behaviors of counselors demonstrated in the helping relationship.

## Optimism

A third assumption of Invitational Learning is that people possess relatively untapped potential in all areas of human endeavor. The uniqueness of human beings is that we have yet to discover any limits on our development.

Optimism—the assumption that human potential is infinite—is fundamental to successful functioning in any helping relationship. No one, not a child, student, parent, worker, patient, client, teacher, manager, or whoever, can choose a beneficial direction in life without hope that change for the better is possible. Counselors who work with clients, educators who teach students, coaches who train athletes, nurses who care for patients, parole officers who supervise parolees, and members of the clergy who lead congregations are successful to the degree that they convey an optimistic belief in the value and capabilities of themselves and other human beings.

From an invitational learning point of view, the single most important thing for anyone who joins in a helping relationship is to have a dream, a vision of what it is possible for people to be: to look at a nonreader and see a reader, to look at a nonathlete and see an athlete, to look at someone who seems unable to handle his or her problems and see someone who can. When professional helpers advance optimistically in the direction of their dreams, success is far more likely to be realized.

A corollary of optimism is the belief that everything counts and nothing in human relations is wasted. Everything we do, and every way we do it, is either helpful or harmful, inviting or disinviting, and either adds to or detracts from the quality of a person's present existence and future potential. Embracing the belief that people possess untapped potential in all areas of human endeavor influences the curricula we devise, the policies we establish, the programs we sponsor, the processes we encourage, and the physical environments we create. Optimism, then, is the belief that human potential, though not always apparent, is always there, waiting to be discovered and invited into realization.

## Intentionality

An invitation can be defined as an *intentional* act designed to offer something beneficial for consideration. Rollo May in *Love and Will* (1969) defined intentionality as the ability people have to link their perceptions with their overt behaviors; he proposed that intentionality is the basis for client intentions and provides the structure by which human perceptions are organized and interpreted. Intentionality enables helping professionals to create and maintain consistently caring and appropriate relationships characterized by purpose and direction.

Invitational Learning proposes that intentionality is a crucial element in any helping relationship; it encourages counselors, teachers, and other helping professionals to develop an awareness of the helpful or harmful potential of every intentional or unintentional action, and to cultivate intentionally inviting attitudes in all their interactions, consistently and dependably inviting well-being in ourselves and others, personally and professionally.

There is also room between the poles of intentionally inviting and intentionally disinviting behavior for behavior that is purposeless, careless, thoughtless, or accidental. Such behavior, while *unintentional,* can be profoundly helpful or harmful in its outcome. Counselors, teachers, coaches, clergy, psychologists, nurses, and allied professionals have the knowledge and skills to offer vital service to others, or to do significant damage. At a practical level, the more intentional we are, the more we are able to "hold the point," to consistently and dependably invite well-being in ourselves and others, personally and professionally.

These four elements of Invitational Learning offer professionals a consistent stance through which they can create personal and professional relationships that encourage the realization of human potential. While there are other elements that contribute to beneficial relationships, these four—*respect, trust, optimism,* and *intentionality*—are essential attitudes to cultivate and maintain for Invitational Learning.

## THEORETICAL FOUNDATIONS OF INVITATIONAL LEARNING

Invitational Learning springs from two theoretical perspectives: *the perceptual tradition* and *self-concept theory.* The perceptual tradition consists of all those systems of thought that attribute primary importance to discovering the way people typically perceive the world and themselves, and the way in which they attribute significance to these perceptions in accordance with their own feelings, desires, and aspirations. A closely allied notion, self-concept, is defined as a learned, organized, and active system of subjective beliefs that an individual holds to be true, that guide behavior and enable each individual to assume particular roles in life.

## The Perceptual Tradition

The perceptual tradition in understanding human behavior and potential consists of all those systems of thought in which efforts are made to view humans as they typically and normally view themselves. The term *perceptual* refers not only to the senses but also to the meanings—the personal significance of an event for the individual experiencing it. These meanings extend far beyond sensory receptors to include all such personal experiences as feelings, desires, aspirations, and the ways people view themselves, others, the world, and their relationships with these phenomena. The basic assumption behind the perceptual tradition is that people behave in terms of how they see things; professional helpers therefore seek to "read behavior backwards," to infer from behavior the perceptual world and belief system of the person who is behaving.

This perceptual tradition contrasts with other theoretical viewpoints such as classical behaviorism, which depicts behavior as a complex bundle of stimuli and responses, or Freudianism, which views our actions as the product of unconscious urges and repressed desires. In the perceptual tradition, primary importance is given to each person's perceived world, rather than to objective behavior or unconscious processes. Since the perceptual tradition maintains that individuals behave in terms of how they see things, healthy human development is enhanced when they understand the nature of their perceptions.

It is clear, moreover, that the belief systems of the helper, in addition to determining his or her own behavior, have a great influence on how students, clients, or patients view themselves

51

and their abilities. In a series of investigations extending more than a decade, Combs and associates (1969, 1971, 1972, and 1978) reported that effective helpers in many professions could be distinguished from less effective helpers on the basis of their perceptual worlds. Across various fields, including teaching and counseling, good helpers tend to see people as able rather than unable, friendly rather than unfriendly, worthy rather than unworthy, dependable rather than undependable, helpful rather than hindering, and internally rather than externally motivated. These studies support two major assumptions of Invitational Learning. First, how professional helpers view themselves, others, and the world largely determines how well they function. Second, the ways in which professional helpers function play a major role in determining the perceptions and eventually the behavior of their clients, students, or patients.

Helpers who use Invitational Learning in their personal and professional lives understand that an individual's behavior may make little or no sense when observed externally, but it becomes logical and understandable when seen from the internal viewpoint of the perceiving individual. These helpers also realize that of all the perceptions we have in life, none is more instrumental in our success or failure than the perceptions we have of ourselves.

*Self-Concept Theory*

Closely allied to the perceptual tradition is the notion of self-concept. This is defined as a learned, organized, and active system of subjective beliefs that individuals hold about themselves, which serves to guide behavior and enables each individual to assume particular roles in life. It is thus a perceptual filter, a moderator variable that influences the direction of behavior. If individuals learn to see themselves as unable, worthless, and irresponsible, they behave accordingly; conversely, if they learn to see themselves as able, valuable, and responsible, they will likewise live up to their own self-concept.

Self-concept is not innate as far as we know; it is learned early in life through repeated perceptions and experiences, particularly with parents, teachers, and significant others. Once it is established, however, it tends toward consistency and stability; individuals strive to behave in ways that are in keeping with their self-concepts, no matter how helpful or harmful to themselves and others. It is an internal guidance system that not only shapes the ways a person views self, others, and the world, but also serves to direct actions and enables each person to take and maintain a consistent stance in life. The more central a particular belief is to one's self-concept, the more resistant one is to changing that belief.

## FOUR LEVELS OF FUNCTIONING

Invitational Learning takes the position that the most logical way to positively influence self-concept development is to explore and improve the myriad messages, formal and informal, intentional and unintentional, that invite people to feel able, valuable, and responsible, and to reduce or eliminate those messages that inform them that they are unable, worthless, and irresponsible. These positive and negative messages are categorized under four major levels of personal and professional functioning.

*Intentionally disinviting* behaviors are those that are deliberately designed to dissuade, discourage, defeat, demean, and destroy. They are therefore the kinds of professional behaviors that Invitational Learning seeks to root out. Such behaviors are most likely to happen when professional helpers become upset and frustrated by circumstances and make nasty or insulting decisions based on these feelings. They sometimes justify them as "being good for them," "getting their attention," "teaching them a lesson," "the only language they understand," "fighting fire with fire," and the like. The Invitational Learning approach is unequivocal in repudiating all such behaviors, and the people, places, policies, programs, and processes that embody or encourage them. It insists on treating all people consistently with respect, regardless of what they have done. In applying Invitational Learning, it helps to keep the **HALT** concept in mind: never make important decisions when you are **H**ungry, **A**ngry, **L**onely, or **T**ired.

*Unintentionally disinviting* people, places, policies, programs, and processes are usually the result of a lack of stance. Because the underlying values of respect, trust, optimism, and intentionality are not clearly articulated or embraced, behaviors are exhibited, policies established, programs designed, places arranged, and processes instituted that are clearly disinviting, although such was not the intent. Professionals who typically function at this level are often viewed as uncaring, chauvinistic, condescending, patronizing, dictatorial, or just plain thoughtless. Examples can be found everywhere: the committee chairperson who always asks a female to take minutes, the school sign that reads NO STUDENTS ALLOWED, the clinic policy of reserving the best parking places for staff, the refusal of an agency to accept checks, the act of pushing papers at one's desk while someone is waiting at the door to speak, or the impoliteness of drinking coffee at a counseling session without offering a cup to the client.

*Unintentionally inviting* behavior is effective but not dependable, because of a lack of a consistent stance. Helpers who perform at this level may be viewed as "natural-born" professionals because they exhibit many of the respecting, trusting, and optimistic qualities associated with Invitational Learning. But they lack intentionality, a conscious perception of meaning, clarity, and significance that would confer consistency and dependability on their behavior, or on the policies, programs, places, and processes they create and maintain. They may know what they do well, but they do not know why they are doing it, or why it works. So when an approach fails to work, they are likely to be confused.

*Intentionally inviting* behavior, people, processes, programs, policies, and places are therefore the goal of Invitational

Learning. To be intentionally inviting personally and professionally toward others, one must be intentionally inviting towards oneself: a high level of personal dignity and self-respect is a precondition for respecting and trusting others. Professional helpers who function at this level exhibit the essential elements of respect, trust, optimism, and intentionality in all they do. Moreover, they do it implicitly and gracefully, without drawing attention to themselves. Recognizing the importance of being intentionally inviting and striving to use this ability in the most artful manner can be tremendous assets in the helping professions.

## CREATING AN INVITING SCHOOL: THE FIVE P'S

In a school or any other organization, everything is connected to everything else. And so, in applying Invitational Learning, everything counts in creating an environment that invites individuals to reach their potential: *places, policies, programs, processes,* and *people.*

*Places,* such as hallways, offices, classrooms, restrooms, waiting rooms, lawns, libraries, commons, and foyers have an extraordinary influence on the perceptions and feelings of those who inhabit them. If professional helpers realize the importance of an inviting physical environment, they are likely to take action so that their physical setting makes their clients feel comfortable, welcome, and appreciated. Schools provide many illustrations of how physical places influence behavior. If a hallway is dingy, the walkways are littered, a bathroom is unpleasant, an office is cold and barren, a classroom is dusty, or a cafeteria is grimy, students will tend to feel uncomfortable, unwanted, and unwelcome despite the best efforts of their teachers or counselors. Conversely, if a physical plant is well maintained, freshly painted, and sensitively designed, with attractive landscaping, bright lighting, new carpeting, inviting messages on signs, and lively bulletin boards that exhibit student work or advertise events, the disposition of students and staff alike will improve accordingly. Creating an attractive and inviting physical setting is the easiest way to begin the process of incorporating the Invitational Learning concept into a school or other organization.

*Policies* refer to the guidelines, rules, procedures, codes, and directives that regulate the ongoing functions of organizations and people. The policies we create reveal the perceptual orientation of the policymakers and communicate powerful messages of trust or distrust, respect or disrespect, and optimism or pessimism. Examples of policies that reflect a lack of trust and respect are frequently found in many schools and other organizational settings: the elementary principal who demands complete silence from children during lunchtime, the counseling center that does not accept personal checks, or buses that leave exactly on time regardless of circumstances. In applying Invitational Learning, counselors and other helpers therefore carefully appraise the procedures used in governing institutions and organizations. For example, professional counselors in diverse settings help parents identify family rules that are reasonable for everyone, or they assist schools in developing policies that encourage student responsibility and participation rather than those that create pervasive anxiety, mistrust, and mindless conformity.

*Programs* likewise have a significant influence on the way people are treated. One reason some programs are less than inviting is that they focus on narrow goals and neglect the wide scope of human concerns. For example, imagine a counseling center program that groups certain individuals together, gives them a label, and treats them all alike. The label itself becomes a stigma that negates the beneficial purposes for which the program was originally created. Similar things happen in schools when tracking programs label students, or when a high school athletic coach "cuts" hopeful young athletes from the team because they are "not good enough" to play. In each case, the resulting stigma can do long-term damage to students' or clients' self-esteem. From an Invitational Learning viewpoint, the school that wins state championships while it discourages many young people from athletics has failed its responsibility. Similarly, the school district that brags of its above-average standardized test scores while accepting a high dropout rate has failed its responsibility. The ends do not and never will justify the means. Conversely, programs that incorporate the assumptions of Invitational Learning include incentive programs such as peer counseling for dropout prevention, faculty mentoring, and other collaborative programs where students, teachers, and counselors all gain by helping and encouraging one another.

*Processes* are embedded in places, policies, and programs, but the term refers more to the context of what is offered than to the content. Extensive research has shown that educators in successful schools value process, establishing behavioral norms of collegiality, professional development, mutual assistance, and ongoing discussion of instruction and curricular improvements among themselves, and cultivating attitudes of respect for all students and attention to their needs in all their interactions. In an invitational school, life is never so hurried that there is no time for a caring, civil, polite, and courteous stance toward everyone. Process involves the recognition that *how* we teach or counsel and *how* we act while doing these things are far more important in the long run than *what* students or clients learn. Frequently, one caring and thoughtful professional helper can make all the difference in encouraging students or clients toward a more responsible and fulfilling attitude toward life.

*People* are the most important part of Invitational Learning and the most challenging; the daily interaction between teachers and students, counselors and clients, and professionals among themselves ultimately determines the success or failure of Invitational Learning. Unfortunately, decisions that have long-lasting effects on people's lives are often made for reasons of effectiveness, efficiency, and conformity that have little or no relationship to the welfare of the people involved. Counselors and teachers who wish to employ Invitational Learning therefore need a sound knowledge of human development, including developmental stages, social and psychological processes, and the principles of learning and behavior, to understand how other significant people in the client's life are contributing to or detracting from his or her development. Assessment of people's dominant level of functioning allows the counselor or other helper to make appropriate decisions about the strategies or approaches that may be beneficial in the helping process. It strongly urges altering, to the extent possible, those influences that directly or indirectly inhibit a person's development, whether these influences derive from other people, or from institutional processes, programs, policies, or places. The goal of Invitational Learning is thus to provide an optimally inviting total environment, both for professional helpers themselves and for those with whom they work.

## THE "FOUR CORNER PRESS"

In addition to (1) identifying the core values of *respect, trust, optimism,* and *intentionality;* (2) presenting the perceptual tradition and the importance of self-concept theory; (3) introducing the five "P's"; and (4) describing the four levels of functioning, Invitational Learning also offers a blueprint for action called the Four Corner Press. Each "corner" represents a vital aspect of successful living. The Four Corners are as follows:

### 1. Being Personally Inviting with Oneself

To show respect, optimism, trust, and intentionality toward others, professionals need to start by becoming inviting with themselves emotionally, intellectually, and physically. By exercising regularly and participating in sports or other recreational activities, we take care of our physical selves. We take care of our emotional well-being by paying attention to our feelings, learning relaxation techniques, and practicing positive self-talk. And we take care of ourselves intellectually by seeking intellectual stimulation through a wide variety of activities that increase knowledge, sharpen thought processes, or improve the overall powers of the mind: taking classes, writing papers, participating in politics, developing hobbies, joining book clubs, and so on.

## 2. Being Personally Inviting with Others

Invitational Learning requires that the feelings, wishes, and aspirations of other people be taken into account. Relationships are like gardens; they require cultivation and nourishment if they are to survive and flourish. Helping professionals understand the importance of sending and receiving positive messages to and from family, friends, and colleagues. Without this social affirmation, we are unlikely to develop at all, except as shriveled fragments of what could have been. Positive experiences in our personal relationships with others contribute significantly to our own personal development and simultaneously enhance our capability of forming beneficial professional relationships.

## 3. Being Professionally Inviting with Oneself

Professionals, including counselors and teachers, spend years in academic training to acquire their skills. But those who accept Invitational Learning are obliged to continue their development beyond their degrees or certificates by updating skills, mastering new techniques, learning new research findings, and locating fresh ways to rekindle the fires of professionalism. Those professionals who return to graduate school, enroll in a weekend workshop, attend conferences, read journals, write for publication, or conduct their own research are keeping themselves alive professionally.

## 4. Being Professionally Inviting with Others

Success in being personally and professionally inviting with oneself leads counselors and other helpers to be professionally inviting with others. Professional helpers should work hard on listening skills, assume responsibility for the helping strategies they choose, and evaluate these selected techniques, modifying them when necessary. They should share talents, form support groups, work cooperatively, network with colleagues, help younger colleagues, maintain optimism, and recognize accomplishment in others.

Chapter 4

# PUTTING IT ALL TOGETHER

by **Garry R. Walz**

Any one of the three approaches to implementing guidance in a school—Comprehensive Guidance Program Model, Teacher Advisor Program, or Invitational Learning and Counseling—can make and is making significant improvements in the assistance provided to students in schools. These three approaches were selected for inclusion in the ERIC/CAPS Crème de la Crème Series (1990) because of their proven effectiveness in schools across the country. Each has a solid conceptual foundation and a guidance strategy that has demonstrated its utility in widely diverse school settings. A detailed and compelling discussion of how each approach can be implemented is also presented in the specific monograph devoted to it. (See References.)

What is unique about this monograph is that it is the first time that the three programs have been presented together. Implicit in the combined presentation are the concepts common to each program. Each approach is not only exemplary in its own right, but all three belong together. It is the intention of this final synthesis to point out not only that they belong together, but also that these three programs are "family"; they go together and can produce exciting and compelling outcomes when adopted as a threesome. A school that uses the concepts and approaches present in all three programs in its counseling program can enhance the effectiveness of each individual program and can also experience a synergistic effect whereby the benefits to students and staff far exceed what could be achieved by any one program alone.

In planning for the implementation of the three programs, however, it is important to focus on how their *combined* use can bring about a special guidance program *synergism.* Undoubtedly, even an unplanned and haphazard use of the three programs will bring benefits to a school. But the real prize is reserved for those school staffs who see the potential benefits inherent in turning the three programs into one program. This chapter explains the potentialities of the "three-in-one" approach. Like the oil known for its capacity to make mechanical items function more smoothly, this three-in-one approach can smooth and improve the functioning of school guidance and counseling programs.

1. *The Comprehensive Guidance Program Model and the Teacher Advisor Program function best in a nurturing and inviting climate—precisely what the Invitational Counseling and Learning approach is designed to provide.*

Most people have had the experience of working on an educational program that looked great on paper but when implemented never produced the expected results. Many times the answer is the human factor, the people responsible for implementing the change or innovation. Many innovation specialists today are calling for a greater attention to the *innovator* (or innovatees) and correspondingly less attention to the innovation. It is the people who are going to *use* the innovation who deserve attention and consideration, not just the physical activity or plan *called* an innovation.

In the context of these exemplary programs it is not just *what* is done but *how* it is done that is crucial. Counselors and administrators who are personally inviting with themselves and others as well as *professionally* and personally inviting with themselves and others will help to create a school climate where both the Comprehensive Guidance Program Model and the TAP can flourish. Only cactuses can grow in sand and then only minimally. All three programs must ultimately be judged by the impact they have upon student growth and development. Students are likely to be only minimally impacted by the outcomes the program espouses unless the behavior of the program's staff is consistent with the intended program outcomes. A staff member who is personally and professionally disinviting can have a severe negative impact upon a program's effectiveness with both students and staff. The "Four Corner Press" presented by Purkey and Schmidt is an excellent model for all program builders and implementers to follow.

2. *The Invitational Learning approach can be instrumental in developing the teacher involvement and cooperation that are essential to the success of the CGPM and TAP.*

The counselor plays a central role in the CGPM and a very important role in TAP, but neither can function well without the spirited involvement and cooperation of the teacher. In TAP especially, teachers because of their image, student contact, and availability may be better suited for the role of student advisors than counselors. The breadth and the comprehensiveness of the CGPM, on the other hand, require that teachers be involved and actively contribute to the achievement of the program's goals through their individual and classroom contact with students. It would therefore strongly behoove anyone intending to use CGPM and TAP to prepare the school staff for participation in these programs.

Helping school staff to identify and respond to the core values of respect, trust, optimism, and intentionality; introducing all staff members to the methods for creating an inviting school by the use of the five P's (places, policies, programs, processes, and people); assisting school staff to understand the four levels of functioning and to assess the level at which they are functioning and what they need to do to become more inviting; and finally using the Four Corner Press to implement successful living—all these factors can have a sizable influence upon the skills and verve brought to their guidance tasks by teachers. Time is one of a school's most valuable assets; it is always limited in a school. If we can bring a value-added component to teacher involvement with students by helping teachers to be more inviting and more helpful to students in planning their careers, resolving personal conflicts, and resisting negative pressures, we

63

have greatly enhanced effectiveness. A teacher may have only 15 minutes with a student, but it can be a time, albeit short, that has lasting positive influence on the student.

3. *The greatest potential for the three exemplary guidance programs described herein is not as disparate, special programs but as an integrated, guidance program thrust.*

Adding innovations to school programs is frequently done the way some people cook—a pinch of this and a pinch of that, and then you taste to see if you've got it just right. Each of these programs can make a significant contribution to a school program—a useful pinch. But their real potential is diminished if a clear recipe isn't followed. Relating each program to the other two programs greatly increases the likelihood of achieving the successful outcomes of any one of the programs. Taken together there can be a real synergism—accomplishing more and having a greater impact than you logically expected. It is difficult, perhaps even unwise, to type each program and suggest what it brings to the "dinner." However, unless you have clearly delineated the range and type of contribution made by each program, your educational potluck may be high on dessert and short on meat and potatoes. Perhaps the following short recipes will help the guidance gourmet plan his/her nutritious spread.

*a. Comprehensive Guidance Program Model.* Counselors and the guidance program are always at risk of marginality and the performance of unessential ancillary services. The significant contribution of the CGPM is to reintegrate guidance into the curriculum and to redefine the counselor's role as one of performing vital duties within a guidance curriculum that is integrated into the educational mainstream of the school. Without this comprehensive design, the brilliance of individual program components (e.g., assessment and testing and career planning) may have only minimal impact upon students. Attempting to build a guidance program without a comprehensive plan is akin to driving over difficult terrain without a map or compass.

   *b. Invitational Learning for Counseling and Development.* School faculties differ enormously in their receptivity to change and their willingness to become involved in new tasks. A new approach has to run the gauntlet of pessimism: "I've tried it before," and other assorted forms of overt and passive resistance. Truly skillful resisters can seemingly actively adopt a new program or practice while covertly ensuring its failure. Crucial therefore to the success of even a very superior program such as the CGPM is the school climate—be it inviting or disinviting. The Purkey and Schmidt Invitational Learning and Counseling Program can assist individual faculty members in assessing their values and adopting behaviors that lead to a more inviting school—one where both faculty and students are committed to helping each other. Interestingly, the positivism generated by the invitational approach feeds upon itself—as staff members become more turned on, they reflect this in their contacts with students who in turn reflect back to the staff the warmth and positivism they themselves have experienced in their interactions with staff. And inviting students make for fewer at-risk and isolated students, and so it goes. It would seem particularly wise on the part of a school, before attempting a major school reform or new program adoption, to build the appropriate climate for the change before introducing the change—a not-so-common bit of common sense that would help to ensure new program effectiveness.

   *c. Teacher Assistance Program.* A well-designed and a well-accepted guidance program may still lack punch or real impact with students because of limitations on counselor time. Certainly a hallmark of the comprehensive guidance program model is the judicious use of staff time and the allocation of priorities to determine who does what. But if contact and interaction with each student (by an adult member of the staff) is an important program goal (as it usually is in a developmental guidance program), the limited availability of counselors becomes a major detriment. This is where TAP becomes such a valuable guidance program component. Preparing teachers to be knowledgeable and caring advisors to students can help to accomplish many developmental guidance goals that would go unmet in a traditional program. Both research and daily experience emphasize the importance of regular student contact with an adult staff member where the focus of the relationship is upon the student, not upon a body of information.

TAP clearly can bring a value-added dimension to the guidance program—economically and with important benefits to the student.

4.  *Typically two to three years is needed for a major guidance program innovation to take hold.*

Even three years is a short time for an innovation to grow sufficient root strength to withstand the negative forces that develop after the initial honeymoon period. Unfortunately, persons not directly involved in the program may have such high expectations that anything other than total success in the first year is unacceptable. The irony in this visceral need for quick success is that the more comprehensive the guidance program model and the more likely the model is to have staying power and lasting benefits to the students and the school, the longer the break-in period is likely to be. Thus, the better programs can well be the ones at risk with the public for quick guidance program fixes.

With the public need for quick and visible progress on newly adopted program innovations, it becomes important, before final program adoption, to establish guidelines as to reasonable program expectations for a three-year span. Longer than three years will dampen people's interest and anything much shorter fails to provide an adequate perspective as to what the significant outcomes will be. It is also wise to build in a standard error factor designating the amount to which the specified outcomes will be over- or undershot.

Wherever possible, it is also highly desirable to state the outcomes in terms that specify what students and/or staff will be able to do that they would be unable to do without the benefit of the specified guidance experience. Expressing the outcomes in meaningful "what can do" statements will make them more understandable and compelling.

5. *A strong commitment to Kaizen—the Japanese concept of continuous improvement—is a must if the content of the guidance program is to remain viable.*

The program that expends too much staff time and energy on program adoption and implementation has little time left for refinement and renewal and is a program headed for early obsolescence and mediocrity. In a world where national and international events impinge spontaneously, unpredictably, and directly on the lives of people in all walks of life, a guidance program that is committed to serving all of its clients must have a system for the rapid renewal and updating of the information it uses. Programmatic decisions can go awry and students can be misinformed if the information transfer to the program is tardy or incomplete. The key word here is *system*—haphazard and unsystematic methods will not do. Students have been misdirected to occupations and educational decisions have been flawed because the test data that drove them was incorrect, and students have missed getting the assistance they needed because "no one knew where to go to get the relevant information."

Unquestionably, the state-of-the-art information resource for counselors today is the Educational Resources Information Center—ERIC. As the largest and most frequently used educational database in the world, it can not only provide counselors with timely information and resources specific to guidance topics, but it can also lead users to bountiful caches of information never intended for counselor use, but highly relevant to the needs of both counselors and clients. Of particular importance is the existence of an ERIC Clearinghouse devoted to the acquisition, processing, analysis, and dissemination of information for counselors—the ERIC Counseling and Personnel Services (CAPS) Clearinghouse at the University of Michigan (2108 School of Education, Ann Arbor, Michigan 48109-1259). The presence of this counseling-oriented clearinghouse ensures that guidance, counseling, and a wide spectrum of other human services topics will be covered in the database.

A major breakthrough in the utility of ERIC for counselors and educators is the availability of ERIC on a compact disk—CD ROM. This feature enables counselors to search the system off-line in the convenience of their homes or offices at very reasonable costs. Equally important, counselors never need say anymore, "I didn't know where to go to get the information." When faced with a major programmatic decision or when assisting a client in exploring a variety of educational and career options, counselors can now quickly retrieve the latest and best information available. Desire is the prime determinant for most counselors today in determining the adequacy of the information they use. Do they have the desire to use the best or will they settle for that which is in hand? All counselors must answer that question individually daily. How they answer it will go a long way in determining how viable a counselor they are.

## CONCLUSION

We have discussed three exemplary guidance programs, each of which has the potential to measurably contribute to a school guidance program. As an integrated threesome, they have the capacity to make significant improvements in school guidance. In a real sense, the programs described here are more cognitive than physical. They focus more on thinking styles, decision processes, and outcome goals than on physical equipment or expensive technology. They are person-driven. They are clearly focused on improving the human condition. Their costs are reasonable by school standards. Most importantly, they can make an important difference in the accomplishments of the staff who use them and the assistance received by the students who experience them.

# REFERENCES

Alexander, W. M., and McEwin, C. K. 1989. *Earmarks of schools in the middle: A research report.* Boone, N.C.: Appalachian State University.

Carnegie Council on Adolescent Development. 1989. *Turning points: Preparing American youth for the 21st century.* Special Task Force Report. Washington, D.C.: Carnegie Corp.

Combs, A. W. 1972. Some basic concepts for teacher education. *Journal of Teacher Education* 23, 286–90.

Combs, A. W.; Avila, D. L.; and Purkey, W. W. 1971. *Helping relationships: Basic concepts for the helping professions.* Boston: Allyn and Bacon.

————. 1978. *Helping relationships: Basic concepts for the helping professions.* 2d ed. Boston: Allyn and Bacon.

Combs, A. W.; Soper, D. W.; Gooding, C. T.; Benton, J. A.; Dickman, J. F.; and Usher, R. H. 1969. Florida studies in the helping professions. *Social Science Monograph.* No. 37. Gainesville, Fla.: University of Florida Press.

Crème de la Crème Series. 1990. Ann Arbor, Mich.: ERIC/CAPS Publications.

Gysbers, N. C. 1990. *Comprehensive guidance programs that work.* Ann Arbor, Mich.: ERIC Counseling and Personnel Services Clearinghouse, University of Michigan.

Jenkins, J. 1977. The teacher-advisor: An old solution looking for a problem. *NASSP Bulletin* 61, no. 410, 29–34.

May, R. 1969. *Love and will.* New York: Norton.

Myrick, R., and Myrick, L. 1990. *The teacher advisor program: An innovative approach to school guidance.* Ann Arbor, Mich.: ERIC Counseling and Personnel Services Clearinghouse, University of Michigan.

National Governors' Association. 1989. *America in transition: The international frontier.* Report of the Task Force on Children. Washington, D.C.: National Governors' Association.

Purkey, W. W., and Schmidt, J. J. 1990. *Invitational learning for counseling and development.* Ann Arbor, Mich.: ERIC Counseling and Personnel Services Clearinghouse, University of Michigan.

Wolfe, D. M., and Kolb, D. A. 1980. Career Development, personal growth, and experimental learning. In *Issues in career and human resource development,* ed. J. W. Springer. Madison, Wis.: American Society for Training and Development.